I0757926

The Girl Who Quit at Leviticus

Also by Suzanne Rhodenbaugh

POETRY
Lick of Sense
The Whole Shebang

CHAPBOOKS
A Gold Rain at Lonelyfarm
Gardening Where the Land Remembers War
The Shine on Loss
Greatest Hits

ESSAYS
The Deepest South I've Gotten

EDITED NONFICTION
Sarah's Civil War: The Edited Diary,
1859-1865, of Sarah Lois Wadley

The Girl Who Quit at Leviticus

poems by

Suzanne Rhodenbaugh

Homestead Lighthouse Press
Grants Pass, Oregon

The Girl Who Quit at Leviticus copyright © Suzanne Rhodenbaugh, 2022, Homestead Lighthouse Press, First Edition

All rights reserved. No part of this book may be reproduced or transmitted in any form without the prior written permission of the publisher.

Library of Congress Control Number: 2021944413

ISBN 978-1-950475-18-6

Homestead Lighthouse Press
1668 NE Foothill Boulevard
Unit A
Grants Pass, OR 97526
www.homesteadlighthousepress.com

Distributed by Homestead Lighthouse Press, Daedalus Distribution, Amazon.com, Barnes & Noble

Cover & Book Design: Ray Rhamey, Ashland, OR
Cover photograph copyright Liz Kahlenberg Bordow

Homestead Lighthouse Press gratefully acknowledges the generous support of its readers and patrons.

Acknowledgments

Ascent "Late Love"

Big Muddy "Highway Loves"

Conestoga Zen (anthology) "Month of the Next Page"
"Poem When a Woman Turns"

The Contemporary Review "Devoutly Wished"

Gardening Where the Land Remembers War
(Two Herons Press chapbook) "On Things Going Right"

Gargoyle "The Girl Who Quit at Leviticus"

Green Mountains Review "North Toward Dying Blues"

Heatherstone Poets Anniversary Edition & New Voices
(Heatherstone Press anthology) (Also published in *The Columbia Book of Civil War Poetry*, Columbia University Press) "The Civil War"

The Hudson Review

"In My Front Yard, Register-
ing People to Vote"
"Peonies and Chrysanthe-
mums," "Tansy," "Asiatic
Lily" and "Mexican Sunflow-
ers" from "Storyflowers"
"This Unholy Mess, My
Body, In Which Consider-
able Spirit Dwells"

The Iowa Source

"From the Aging Day"
"White Garden at the End
of My Summer"

Kansas City Star

"Cold Time Testament"

The Laurel Review

"Country Music"

Michigan Quarterly Review

"Florida Water Sources and
the Best Seeing"

Poetry East

"Iris," "Mallow," and
"Closed Moonflower
Opens" from "Storyflowers"

River Styx	"Science, Art, Urban Policy" "The Things I've Put in My Mouth" "The Views of the Widow's Daughter"
The Shine on Loss (Painted Bride Quarterly chapbook)	"Ecology of Luck"
South Florida Poetry Review	"Garden, Wood and Shore"
Southern Poetry Review	"Morning's Journey to Thought"
Spillway	"Letter to a Student on the Shimmering"
Swivel	"The Four Basic Town Groups"

Contents

To the saving graces: Tom and my friends

Garden, Wood and Shore

I glance to the moon,
that student all day long
of the sap rising, the creatures moving to the buds
slew-footed, and slow-haunched.

At the oak's first fork, raccoons
survey the accidental tulips
pushing up the lawn. Lilies grow
thick in the curved bed,
old daffodils and rhubarb rise up.

I smell honeysuckle tangle in the wooded
drop of the yard, feel toe-jam
oozing in my summer toes in April.

Toes point and flex to feel the boulders
piled to make a jetty to the lighthouse.

God keeps up the crosshatch,
says beachlines, woodlines, overlap for all
His rising peopled world,
possum playing possum on the lean-to,
old chicken shit under fallen branches,
forsythia strident anyway and underneath it –
johnny jump-ups.

The sap and root,
stem crossing stem, the tumbled
goddamn mess, to crawl with longing
into the loose nest, to have it all.

Country Music

Long time we've been not having,
your hands not touching my breasts.
We still don't know each other's rhythm
though the melody is strong and familiar,

a song we keep humming to ourselves.
In all we keep not having,
we haven't held each other, or tried.
I haven't cupped you in my hand,

haven't told you anything in any
pink sweat, haven't
touched or tasted or bit or sucked
or received you, or loved you.

Haven't, all the seasons.
We've kept refined as young folk
who want so strongly
and feel things the keenest

alone. We're drawing out
not having, making it last.
I love the tune.
Someday I'll sing it out loud.

Song of the Traveler's Wife

Oh yes and I will be here
by the front porch latchkey
or I'll wait on the stoop
or in the bushes – you say where.

I'll reckon the time of the month
by how much of the moon
has gone away.

I'll cup my hands around
some green apple tea –
I'll wait.

I could place my hands
on the mound where you said
at least one grey hair should grow,
that time you told me I'm well-preserved
and I said, like a mummy, huh?

I'll climb the stairs to the room
over the porch that looks east.
I'll wave to the watermen.

I'll construct a widow's walk
for growing old in New England.

I'll snap out of it.
I'll carry split logs
two by two
to the round iron hoop

I can sit on
while I wait
for you.

Oh yes. I intend to be
taken to the Dark Town
Strutters Ball – I'll wait.

Religious Preference

I don't want to feed
at the trough of love.
I don't want to wait or stand.

I don't want to kneel
before a prostrate God,
or a manageable tick
in a blurred white sky.

I want a sky that's hot and blue,
God in pants, and full of the devil.

On Things Going Right
to Tom

Kids OK and sometimes good, relatives not
running amok with crises – no one's
died for almost a year. And we're solvent.
No stitches, wrenched backs or failed transmissions.

The roof isn't leaking now, the 80 year furnace
hasn't blown up yet, there's been no repeat
of cars out of control hitting the house
nor another burglar, bout of termites,

broken water line or shoulder, no more
biopsies, no more jobs gone belly-up.
EKG abnormal although, as I told the doctor,
this heart looks funny, but it will keep.

It'll keep a garden thrumming with care,
supper spicyhot on the ready and my love
unto your body – it will keep
unhurriedness, and conversation meant.

Late Love

Last night he called from Fargo and I said
"Fargo! You're in such a mysterious place!"
"Fargo?" he said, "Fargo, North Dakota?
It's just a plain town on The Great Plains."

I said "Oh but I remember
poems by James Wright and Thomas McGrath.
Doesn't a train run through?
Wasn't it a crossroads during the Depression?"

He hesitated. The way I make romance out of sorrow
I think startles and sometimes offends him.

But he thought to say of Fargo, "Well, yes,
I guess it was a crossroads.
There's a beautiful old station.
It's a senior center now."

"A *senior center?*"
        "Yes."

I went quiet then. I wanted the old station
abandoned to moonlight.

I said "I'm glad
it's still of some use.
I'm glad it's not lying in ruin."
We put our phones in their cradles.

I walked out then to the garden.
I imagined he walked late too
under the same old moon
shining on our white iron glider,

where some summer evening hence
we'll sip white wine and say
Fargo goes on by simple trying –
something that mysterious, that plain.

White Garden at the End of My Summer

Almost every evening, though not more than one bloom
is granted, the moon vine out back will blossom.
I go to the garden and stare.

If it can make one bloom, why not more?
Why can it not be covered, a bounding
full-blossoming vine?

If I took what has been festering, the persistent
eggshells and stinging onion skins,
the slimy tomatoes and coffee grounds and rinds

and basted the roots of the moon vine
with the gloppy rot, would I get more
moon vine blossoms?

The size of a hand,
one ghostly trumpet only?
My God, I'm trying to listen.

Month of the Next Page

The languor of the gardens and the yards
ignored all through late summer
starts amid September. It's a languor of ardor.

The month gives over bounty, in a sprawl, exhausted
August in the arms of brilliantly-detached October's
autumn studies – maples taking on orange,
star leaves of the sweetgum burnished gold.

In the bittersweet hubbub of September,
violet heads of phlox fade but still will stay,
hydrangea turns mahogany.

September is the year's odalisque,
the month my glamorous mother was born.

And September is the year's nexus,
when I gave up my newborn daughter.

Cold Time Testament

More savage and more staid
is the ornamental ironwork God
wrought from winter trees,
foreground for a sky
hidden through the softer seasons.

Only in winter the blood and coral copper
sky, sky of color some god wrought.

From the Aging Day

I lose the sting of blowing snow,
the crunch beneath my foot. I can't recall
the piney woods in fall
nicked with surprises – the blood tomato
mushrooms, or the differing strains
of light by season. These things

leave me, as on a pine
board a stew steaming
ready for the family
is not the satisfaction that it was,
and I forget the ease
of rest, the smell of love, the joy

persisting by my back stoop:
the single untended fiery tulip.

STORYFLOWERS

Iris

Once I was all lips and tongue.
Now I am a fist.

Peonies and Chrysanthemums

The size and virtual heft
of grapefruits,

the peonies soft, dense, smooth,
like the sweet rumps of pink ponies.

Mums come later, for the football fest
corsages of the town's two top high schools.

They can take glitter, furry twisties
and bows.

Like moms, they are strong
and last much longer.

Malva Hollyhock

The lavender of chicken feed sacks
dabbed with white by a Sunday painter:

crisp four-petaled flowers
impervious to bugs.

Has anyone seen Grandma?

Spiderwort

Purple discs on long grey-green stalks
happiest pushing up through other flowers:
floral buttinskys.

Gladiolas

Between her emptied house
and the occasional passing stranger,
in the generous bed
of the several grassy acres
facing the rural road,
the farmer's wife plants bulbs.

They braid into tall folded blossoms
coral, white, yellow, red and pink:

cheery swordlike flowers
favored for funerals.

If small furred torches

were brash in a hot sundown, fuchsia
orange and gold: celosia.

But if pale pink fire in a silent twilight,
and a certain modesty prevailed: astilbe.

Tansy

Fuzzy yellow buttons push through
luxuriant ferny plumage.

(In the madame's furs
the peasant's still present.)

Asiatic Lily

Handsome candelabrum
lacks for nothing.

Begonia

Waxen leaf like a much-buffed dining room table,
and a sound like a servant gone away
or bid to leave.

Mexican Sunflowers

Monarchs love these purest orange

petites with their overblown leaves:
redheaded bridesmaids in green taffeta dresses
ruffled, bowed and bustled.

Bees and hummingbirds also come nuzzlin'.

Petunias

Droopy Daliesque trumpets,
until the sun plays them
up.

Mallow

This giant hibiscus could court
the portly, woo the zaftig or bodacious,
but chiefly serves the under-leaf.

Its plate-size flowers offer little creatures
wrinkled velvet shelter.

Closed Moonflower Opens

Green-toned sugarcone,
dollop of vanilla on top.

Sun licks it, nightfall kicks in:
opulent moon on the vine.

Red yarrow

Tiny blossoms nearing burgundy
cluster into their own bouquets,
each eye the size of a golden bug:

England somehow, during The Middle Ages.

Ecology of Luck

I gave my lapis lazuli, my mustard seed.
I gave away my Israel rock with the gold
fingers reaching up through it.
You might think my luck's run out,
or that I got it back in plenty
from the giving, and the need.

Not so. I'm looking for new luck to give.
What paper scraps and slugs of coal I keep
rest here on my books, taking on dust
and history, waiting for perfect receivers,
like the alligator skull I found,
smooth red-speckled stones I garnered.

I want to take on luck like cargo,
ship to friends all over the country.
The stainless teapot I resurrected
will go, some day, to someone I love.
This isn't the Jesus spirit.
I don't expect my luck to multiply

by giving out. It's more like mailing
a human head in a cardboard box
for the shock of it, and the reminder:
Salome with her own head on the platter,
a shipment to John the Baptist.
He will take the brain and eat it,

take the feast of what I've felt and make it
mercy, feed on it, and spit the seeds.
They'll grow into gourds and melons,
be harvested and dried. Shellacked
and painted with turtles,
they'll catch, at least, God's eye.

Devoutly Wished

Some days a drunk is lying in the gutter,
utterly revealed, and this brings woe, a little.

And you want, in your heart's keep,
some shadows – giant ones on walls,

raggedy and scary. I tell you a crow
is sitting on your shoulder,

waiting with a sense of humor
and a beak to rip your heart out.

That crow's swoops and enormous cries
can be seen and heard all seasons.

And one day, the cockeyed back stoops
by the rail tracks and the pathetic swords of weeds

will cause a large sob to rise in your chest.
On the 7:10 to Manhattan

you'll stand and say clearly, *This hurts.*
You commute in a sharkskin suit

but in its warp and woof are eons –
you're connected and swimming is good,

it's good. Someone has to be the heavy.
But photograph yourself.

Pin the picture on the mantel and look:
the photo, the shooter and the shot at

merged in one. And do the opposite:
take all images and burn them.

And try to keep the Visigoths alive by the fjords.
Tell how the boats broke up and the black winds blew –

we need reminding, often. Daily,
you arrange deck chairs on the Titanic.

You line them up just right.
When everything is perfect,

you see how deep the water,
how dark, how goddamn cold.

You want to dive in and be dramatic,
or drowse in the chairs till noon.

But you will go by a man's way.
You will lead the others to safety,

you will kindly lift them down,
taking first those pixilated, furiously so.

In you, the seasons and the days and nights
have crowded up and made you notice time.

Once you walked through the Crimea,
through all the smoke,

the haphazard drumming and the flaying
you heard the nightingale, and the orphan.

The Edge of American History

I look out on the North Atlantic
salt vat, a brine that gets its feed,
ocean full of our detritus –
spats and snoods from the Titanic,
arms and testicles from The Great War
floating in it still and maybe slave bones,
maybe scrimshaw carved by the whaling men.

In 1943 sailors' bodies washed up here –
they fed it. Long ago Blackbeard fed it. I saw
a helicopter full of human men feed this water
calls our pilgrims and our slaves, our mariners.

A North Atlantic hungers for us all – our stew,
our conglomeration. The slop of our history
abides in the sentient whales' repository.

These at least were my thoughts
in the loneliness of The Outer Banks.

And after witness: a U.S. Army Chinook
did fall to its death before me at Cape May Point.

Lonely too at Chincoteague,
Deer Isle of Maine, and many points between,

I walked to the edge of the water
as if to gather the lost in my arms.

Then came a winter, in a saltbox on our coast,
I set one place at the table. At the thought

of sentient sounding whales
some days I grew near-joyful.

Mostly though, from a widow's walk,
I only called for simple help – for company, for talk.

Once, bent on a winter
day at The Sound, I walked at Seaside Park.

My thighs were stiffening.
My eyes were streaming.

Behind me was a mountain of landfill
transported by hysterical gulls.

Offal stuck to my boots.
I walked and must have said my thoughts

out loud, for a man
shouted at me then:

You crazy bitch! Who gives a flying fuck?
He winked, gave me the finger,
and in his hut
of cardboard, hunkered down.

North Toward Dying Blues

It's not eternity I want: not a freefall
I think I've earned by hardscrabble birth
or the way flesh loosens, and flaps.
I'm not greedy. I'll stop at any roadside
stand for barbeque, ribs slapped
in their thick sauce. I don't have to walk
down to the muck-bottomed lake,
my legs two glorious divining rods.

It can be New England: cold,
brooks there what I called creeks.
It can be stones hurting my insteps
though I grew up expecting
mud between my toes, and a much longer time
to ease into the sitdown for a meal,
some drawn-out talk,
and sleepfall, that old bottleneck guitar.

Poem When a Woman Turns

for Barbara Karpas

The garden's blowsy with yesterday's rain.
The cosmos beaten to the ground
grow fulsome, and will right themselves.

That Englisher light
enlivens color in the zinnias, and the mums
strengthening for a fall flaunting.

The muted past-glory
blossoms of hydrangea
grow arresting in the greyer light

and we can see, far
from its last blooming, the autumn clematis
promising a show in the gloaming.

Instance

> "We all know of moods in which two beams con-
> verge, and we experience an overwhelming certainty
> of meaning *and* of objective reality."
>
> *-- Colin Wilson*

About a week before Christmas I stopped in the grocery store
to look over a large display of potted Norfolk Island pines,
each about three feet tall. Another woman was looking too
and I pointed out to her what seemed the greenest and best-formed
of the little pines. She said, "Yes, but it has a broken branch."

I lifted the branch and saw it was bent but not fully broken,
and said to the woman, quite near me now, "Maybe because this one
has a broken wing, you can love it more." She looked up, startled,
and we were both quiet for several moments. Then she said "Yes"
and chose it.

Highway Loves

I love how strangers on the highway
flash their lights to kindly say
"Smokey's up ahead – look out."

How in Virginia the signs will mystify,
as in "No unlawful fires
after four o'clock."

And in Connecticut the state
will take no blame:
"Drive this road at your own risk."

Someone has put red noses on all the deer
crossing signs in Pennsylvania,

and in The South, you never arrive
at Stuckey's, though billboards line
the way all trip beside

the whirligigs, the florid
chenille spreads for sale and the ads
for pecans. On a slight rise on somebody's farm

or lonely stretch, telephone poles
have been made into Calvary.
And as much as humans and the Lord allow,

dogs lean out car windows
and grin in the wind.

The Four Basic Town Groups

Whiskey   Devil's Garden, Florida
               Brass Castle, New Jersey
               Brasher Center, New York
               Shallowater, Texas
               Coarsegold, California
               Rough Rock, Arizona
               Wild Horse, Colorado
               Horseshoe Bend, Idaho
               Wagon Mound, New Mexico
               Ninemile Camp, Hawaii
               Major's Place, Nevada
               Fort Defiance, Virginia

Ham   Cooter Point, Louisiana
               Hogshooter, Oklahoma
               Slab Fork, West Virginia
               Fry Canyon, Utah
               Goose Creek, South Carolina
               Blue Lick Springs, Kentucky
               Possum Grape, Arkansas
               Beanblossom, Indiana
               Bewelcome, Mississippi
               Craggie Hope, Tennessee
               Social Circle, Georgia
               Heartsease, North Carolina

Cornbread   Homewood, Alabama
Sweet Air, Maryland
Morning Sun, Iowa
Grainfield, Kansas
Center Barnstead, New Hampshire
Chimney Point, Vermont
Pepperbox, Delaware
Butternut, Wisconsin
Applegate, Oregon
White Cottage, Ohio
Blue Eye, Missouri
Plainview, Nebraska

Grits   Nightmute, Alaska
West Sound, Washington
Braintree, Massachusetts
Watch Hill, Rhode Island
North Star, Michigan
Winter Harbor, Maine
Gales Ferry, Connecticut
Starkweather, North Dakota
Moose Lake, Minnesota
Wolf Point, Montana
Crowheart, Wyoming
Black Lane, Illinois
Bonesteel, South Dakota
Elders' Ridge, Pennsylvania

In My Front Yard, Registering People to Vote

If I just sit placidly reading
I can't put my voting mojo on them
but if I smile and look intently at the folks
waiting at the light, some wave
or give a thumbs up or a victory sign
and only one in weeks has shouted
Trump! A few even stop to register
or change address. I get to watch

the clouds changing and the fine Victorian park
across the street, and the shrubs and flowers
of my front yard's effulgence, me nestled between
the autumn sedum and the nine bark,
the nandinas and the mugho pine,
the barberries, marigolds, dogwood.
And my single giant pumpkin
in a big pot of orangey lantanas.

Many people the dogs are walking
seem distracted or harried, or pointedly ignore
a grey-haired woman with a clipboard,
but even across the side street
dogs raise their heads and sniff and look
my way to say: "You've changed the world
at this corner." I do so wish
alert enthusiastic dogs could vote.

Science, Art, Urban Policy

Arthur's angelwing carp, Goldie, has dropsy.
Her mouth is almost in the gravel, her long
translucent waving ("inefficient," Arthur says)
tail and fins are skyward. Says Arthur, "Goldie's
fish bladder got off-kilter from a bacterium
I tried to alter by injecting antibiotics
into the water. This cured the disease
but not the dropsy." (Arthur is a scientist.)

Sybil says, "You should put Goldie to death.
Should bury her in the backyard by your wife's
intense blue forget-me-nots." (Sybil is a poet.)

Says Arthur, "Dropsy isn't so bad."
Sybil says, "How do we know? She's definitely got
discomfort, maybe even pain. She may in fact
be near death." "Goldie loves human interaction,"
says Arthur, "look how she welcomes my hand."
Sybil says, "What choice does she have? It's upside
down all day and night or you reaching in
to right her. What's she going to opt for?"

While their spouses go to a yard sale featuring
African masks and ski boots,
Sybil and Arthur discuss Goldie.

They never reach a definitive position.
They do agree to love the Amtrak policy whereby,
for a change back to Standard Time, all the trains
in America stop at 2 a.m. for one hour
"in order for time to catch up."
"*Beautiful* notion," says Sybil and Arthur agrees,
though he's a little mystified, maybe.
Sybil is mystified for sure: she has no idea

what she means. Meanwhile, at the heavily-
trafficked junction in the smoke-blue kitchen,
alone in a cloudy tank, Goldie still has dropsy.

The Views of the Widow's Daughter

I.

In our house, things match correctly and we don't say "ain't." My mother knows how to act. This way, despite the Rushings' dirt-eating kids – there are too many of them, too close together, my mother says so – and the Hondurans being foreign, and Billy and Jimmy's mother being vague – she's like a loose strand of hair – we're sure of things and have good taste. We're definite.

I'm the only girl at school in Buster Brown oxfords but this is because my mother knows more about growth and support and lining up the bones right.

I use a lot of bandaids not because I play sports, I don't too much, but I go to the playground and fall off my bike. It's fascinating to look at scars. The best scar in our family belongs to my oldest sister, who jumped off the garage roof onto a piece of sheet metal standing upright in the backyard for God knows what reason. That was back before I existed.

To be lost and gone forever, sometimes I throw my Buster Browns up in the peppertree but they don't stick there because they're heavy, and my only tree isn't high enough.

In the shade of the peppertree I put rubber bands on my shoebox and strum, many times, beautiful tunes.

When I'm older my hair will be all possible colors because I'll bleach a streak at each of my temples. Right now my hair falls without grace from the crown of my head, so that my mother pulls it tightly back and with rubber band keeps it held. Rubber bands have many uses.

II.

My mother and I are refined. We have slender bone structures, good ones, the best kind. All the mess around us doesn't make us common.

Our alley is green like a corridor and not a city alley, not remotely approaching. From there I spy people in their kitchens, back doors, backyards. Their garbage cans are scummy. A lot of them don't have lids and things spill out, although nothing ever horrible, not yet.

To keep out peeping toms and marauders, I shut the windows and lock them. I pull down all the shades. I squeeze the blackheads from my mother's back. I pluck the hairs from her chin.

I have a birthmark the size of a dime on my shinbone, and a crater scar between my eyebrows. I am the youngest, the last one left at home, and my mother's only reason for living. Otherwise, I am unmarked in a permanent way. The hair on my head is so far thick, wavy, dark and long. If I shaved it, I could make a rope.

Lester Rushing died from a bullet. Another neighbor from an ulcer. Mr. Brown just walked to the end of the block, put dynamite caps in his mouth, and blew his head off. My father took a night to die. He was in a sanitarium, unseen. That was long ago.

In our neighborhood, all the women live. This is deadly accurate and true although I remain confused about whether, to be a survivor, I must first live and marry.

III.

Greenland, from the air, is only black and white and nowhere green. I saw it with my own eyes in the days when I traveled, worked and lived.

On the ground it's fjords: rivers of layers of turquoise ice. The buildings, land and men have no particularity. The frozen rivers which might crack and heave are what I remember foremost. Also, the abandoned hospital. During World War II the Allies put there men missing all their limbs, men with half-heads, and so on: all those who, if sighted by the public, would hurt the cause.

At the time I witnessed this desolation – it was the era of Vietnam – I was with a man named Hawk and a man named Marger running Scotch from the British Isles to the lonely Danes on Greenland. I'd joined them from Jerusalem, where the eyes of the Virgin Mary in the Church of the Holy Sepulchre are exactly like my mother's: purely blue, unstriated, tearless, and always open. My irises have the coward's yellow ring and yet I'm not without experience.

I lived with one man in a garage facing an alley. We were poor, distraught, and violently alive. Another man, of the so many I knew carnally, was a powerful leader of civil rights. He'd call me late at night just out of the blue and say: catch a cab, come to my motel room. Though his penis was a billy club and it hurt to receive him, I did. Sometimes he made me hide while he bought guns for Sparta.

I met my husband during my days in the coalfields. He called from the Union: we met by voice. When eventually we came into each other's presence, he saw I was not the woman in workboots he'd visualized, but more a girl. I wore unbleached muslin, cotton lace, and blue lawn. My feet were strapped in little brown sandals.

After that, I had to parse my living.

IV.

It has been clear to me I had to venture out not once but many many times, and clear I had to come back.

My myopia has greatly worsened, to which has been added, with no overall improvement in vision, the countervailing tendency to see poorly up close, and dry eyes – the latter two signs, of course, of age.

My dry eyes – all paradox – mat in the mornings.

It was a bright day in April when, sure of no frost on the steps, I slipped and most heavily fell. My husband said my vision accounted for my falling. He said my missteps were not clumsy, but a simple failure to see. I've only recently learned *come a cropper* describes such a headlong fall.

I live now in a more defined, contracted space. My movement is limited. Even when people come to me, I don't necessarily see them.

But it's enough. What's jumped in the holes of my eyes remains. I've taken in things everywhere I've been, frozen them into frames, and held them: the green cliffs falling straight to the sea above the beaches in Nova Scotia, where the tide is the most powerful in the world, the deep enveloping feather beds of Iceland.

In my own country I was compelled north to The Adirondacks, The White Mountains, The Colorado Rockies, The Sierra Nevada, Denali in Alaska – the list goes on. Most cold places, I have been.

My husband wanted the cold, and I went along with him. Though in point of fact, even before I met him, I wanted white land stripped of details.

V.

For all this, I love the heat. I come from a swampy place of Spanish moss, dense undergrowth, snakes, sinkholes, and a pervasive wetness. Swamps are not to my liking – I fear them – but nothing can belie the formative.

I am back to where alleys are green. In northern places, alleys tend to be narrow and paved, and otherwise bereft. Here, the alleys are alive. From them you can see more truth about the people. Were it not for the danger, I would use alleys exclusively.

My window looks out on a broad green alley. Once I went there to look for evidence of poison, for my white cat died. I could not find it, and neither could an expert. He said a death such as hers might be from a trace of poison, or from hidden internal injuries – no way to know.

Cause unknown is a hard basis on which to grieve, but it is often the case. I buried her with a marble rock I found crunched against a fence. I thought her bones would make the ground richer, but so far the dirt is compacted and stony, and neither the white lily nor the cleome nor the sweet alyssum has flourished. It may be that with more time and heat, they will.

VI.

I have dark circles under my eyes. This puts me in the company of sufferers, although a man once told me my eyes are so light he could go by their avenue through history and time all the way back to the fjords.

This man was black. To him, my eyes meant danger. He saw the wide round light blue eyes of the potential perpetrator of suffering.

Another black man told me my eyes are the color of the lakes of Mississippi. He was a Mississippi man, and loved his home.

These seeings and characterizations do not after all amount to much. Romantics say such things when they want to make love, or hurt.

They're good to turn over in my mind, though, as if my mind held its own turquoise monkey rock, or chunk of lapis lazuli, or a sapphire like my mother wore, or the zircoin of my childhood, and turned it every which way for the facets of light and the feel.

Plainly, my eyes are not all that light. They're more a murky, muddy blue, a stone blue, a grey. Their lashes are scant and unremark-able, their eyebrows nothing to write home about.

The eyes have been a problem – there's no denying that – but they've been serviceable. I've looked out at the world through them, and I've been able to see.

Tennessee Williams said the eyes are last to go out. The exact way I phrase it is: when the face closes down unto death, the eyes are the last to go out.

Letter to a Student on the Shimmering

It's summer now: hot
where you live.
Where I am,
the season comes slower.

You write like you're
a swimmer, plunging in
and varying the stroke.
I turn the pages over

to words in your last letter:
Vale, cum magnus amor.
This can't ever be
but is a sweet year's

summing up. You're a man
of thirteen. I'm a woman past forty.
I have to row away now,
but I want you to know: I'm fully

sure you can swim.
And I too felt the fire in the lake.

Morning's Journey to Thought

in memory of Donald Justice

I step one moored rowboat to another,
the boats tied end on end
in a tide neither high nor low.
I reach the last boat linked to the harbor.

No knowing then.
The smell of quince might come,
or the train sound out of the grey rock face
across the bay, or the turn of leg

my mother shows on a stair, the swell
of calf and narrow ankle,
despite how ancient she's growing.
I could go anywhere. I do. I set to drift,

wanting to be carried and be rocked
though not quite out of sight of land.
One morning in a hundred
something rises – a mermaid

with immense brown nipples,
or a grinning psychic porpoise
who looks like me, or then again a net,
a discernible dead life in it,

by mistake. The boats
bump against each other from the dock,
through intermediaries, to the last far boat
where always nothing gently beckons.

The Civil War

A column of lemon sky lit one hill.
Heaven to earth it divided the blue
and all the movement was downward.

Slimming runnels foraged
for a streambed in the bracken.
Rills of dirt slid down.

She picked her way downhill.
Burrs and stalks in the undergrowth
pricked and rasped her fetlocks.

Rocks dislodged tumbled.
As the declivity steepened
she fell headlong.

The mare without her rider
lay down in the valley of the valley.

People of the South

We got a hole in our soul: slavery.

We got experience of defeat
and the feel of a foot on our neck.

We got people mean and sweet.
Sometimes they're in the same body.

We got land that's sand or swamp.

Or clay or delta dirt or mud – we got most
every kind of land.

And up out of that land, three kinds of music:
country, blues and jazz.
Plus zydeco, rock and roll, bluegrass, gospel,
work songs, railroad songs
and more. Two are blue inside.
Most all are black and blue from use and roots.

We got history. We got knowledge of history. We got
ignorance, bone deep.

We got literature, the country's most distinctive.

We got a thousand ways to tell a story
and can't tell a simple one
without understory, without background,
without making a point of the fact that

AnnaRuth's second husband was first cousin once removed
to Jim Tucker from Tifton, remember he had that bad accident
just about killed him? This was subsequent to him
starting an insurance company with Buddy Parsons,
that sorry excuse for a man married Ernestine Ledbetter
straight out of school and left her right soon after.

We got no-count. We got clock-watchers. We got saintly.
We got lawyers, surgeons, government workers, football coaches,
revolutionaries and daily people. We got lizards, gators, scorpions,
panthers, bears and snakes. We got pythons
in the Everglades now: imports run amok.

We got heat. We got mosquitoes, tornadoes, hurricanes.
Black ice and ice you can see.

We got religion, even if our mamma made it seem
Jews and Catholics are exotic.
Muslims and Sikhs never entered her head
and forget Buddhists, Hindus, atheists – your major exotics.

We got a church or a field or an intersection
where a child idly sings
an old country hymn of peacedness
imagined and extended, rhythmical and unforgettable,
learned from a grandmother hailed from St. Mary's, Georgia
just north of Jacksonville, maiden name was Johnson.

That child yearns for what's true and what's real, and what can never be gainsaid. We got that kid, we got that kid in our hearts.

The Girl Who Quit at Leviticus

A blue spot shone on the Methodist Youth Camp
counselors acting out
Smoking, Drinking, Cussing,
sin blue as a saloon. In my ponytail

I left the chapel sobered and sucked in
my breath with resolve
for going through the Bible in one year.
I set out and didn't flag for months.

The Devil, who wasn't big with Methodists,
never took me. There was no Big Fall.

Just that my peppertree, where I climbed high
to read, seemed to call for
The Black Stallion,
The Return of the Black Stallion.

Looped on a slender limb
I read until the night came down.

I went farther and farther
from The Good Book into tales
of mystery and slaughter,
into love and dark achievement,

whereby I missed the angels,
and the pale horse of *Revelations.*

Florida Water Sources and the Best Seeing

Headwater. Mouth
of the river. So hard to understand
where it starts and where it ends,
to remember the headwater
tiny, a trickle, a bubble
up out of dry ground,
and the mouth – wide as a country.

With greater ease I learned
the dark swimming moons
beside my rowboat in Crystal River
were seacows. Manatees.
Their bulbous undulating masses
huge enough to tip the boat
were live. I couldn't see their eyes
or know their heads from ends
but I knew not to swim,
nearblind, in that river.

And so I turned to sinkholes,
barren funnels filled with bright water
bubbling from the underground springs.
Clear. Even with bad eyes.
I swam along the tops in teeshirt
and cut-off jeans, wide-opening
eyes to the clear cold water.

I heard one sinkhole
swallowed a whole car,
and feigned to take a town –
a sudden large thing. But that's not
what I knew of sinkholes.

Mine was one deep V at the edge of a swamp.
Few people came there. Rocks weren't set around
and there was no formal sign.
It was just a known place –
you could go for free with the boy you loved.

Out of a muggy day you'd dive right in
and down you'd go,
getting cool and getting clean, knowing
it had no outlets and no end
you could hold your breath
and watch the bright swaying
things in this clear water, eyes wide open.

Must Have

I walked in timid, said
"I've got these bites."
I just stood there
afraid the nurse'd catch on
how I got a thousand-plus
bites on my backside - a lot
clustered on my neckback,
shoulders, fanny, thighs,
but roping too round to my front.
I even had bites on my toes.

I think she said "Oh my! How
did you get these bites?"
I think I said
"Lot of mosquitoes
out behind Humanities -
I was reading there."

She didn't mention how
dark it'd been to read,
or how ugly the scrub was
out behind Humanities.
Just took wads of cotton,
dipped them in the alcohol,
daubed the one-thousand
bites one at a time.

I don't think HE went to the infirmary.
Must've caught the bus itching.
Must've itched the hour and a half
back to town. Must've smelled bad too
and looked bad – dirty, kind of
torn up. Must've thought of me,
must've thought he loved me

awful bad to go out to the scrub
palmetto, lie in the poison
oleander and the anthills.

Must've thought he'd gone crazy.
Must've wondered what got him.
Must have itched.

The Things I've Put in My Mouth

Outside Macon, red clay on Zebulon Road
in hellish heat I hardly noticed,
being a refined inward Southron child.

Berries. I might have died.
The pine needles I picked up.
Twigs and straw and blades of grass.

Cheers and prayers and food – chicken fried
loud in lard, okra and tomatoes, baked ham.
Beans and corn and catfish.

Curls of chocolate. The ends of my hair.
The edge of my turtleneck.
The ridiculous accents of French,

the German clomp, and Hebrew,
like hawking up phlegm.
Cigarettes, 3 packs a day, 36 years.

Iced tea by the barrel, wine by the bucket.
Bloody marys, joints, a few filched uppers.
The swollen cocks of men of course

and babies' fingers and babies' toes,
not to mention advice and general jawing,
a spate of words spewed out in every form but opera.

Once, the Anglo-Saxon line in a sad, chocked sonnet.
And the howled vowels of hymns.

This Unholy Mess, My Body, In Which Considerable Spirit Dwells

The eye doctor says my eyeballs are extraordinarily
long: they go far into the back of my head.
He's a man I gave my only copy of an anthology
featuring eyes, including mine, on the cover,
and now he's appalled. I lamely counter
"Poets are supposed to see deep."

My regular doc explains the abdominal aorta
is like "a garden hose through the middle of the body."
(Here's a man speaks my language.) But in my case
it ends in ruin, an aqueduct crumbling at its endpoint.

My heart man says a blip on the EKG indicates
"left bundle branch block,"
which is damn hard to say!
It may mean my heart is erratic,
but then whose isn't?

As for sacroiliac, a word I thought a joke
made up to rhyme with "out of whack,"
my left one has gone outlaw. And this is weird
because it's not a *thing* but a *space*, where other parts
hook up. Hiatal hernia, hypothyroidism, hypertension,
plano pilaris, arthritis, sometimes a fall
into vertigo, even traces of the terrible
Mask of Pregnancy I had over 50 years back.

And yet standing on these flat feet I can still cook
prodigious meals. I've cooked thousands in my long life.
And with my extremely myopic, post-cataract,
still-cloudy eyes, I've read thousands of books.
(Most of them during the pandemic.)
I can still heft 40 pound bags
of manure and mulch and clean,
over time, a three story house.

This body has carried sleeping children to bed.
It's climbed a hillside at dawn to irrigate young pines
on Kibbutz Ginegar, skinny-dipped in New Hampshire's
Swift River. It's hitchhiked alone at night from Vermont
to New York City, just to see Bobby Weintraub one more time.
It's won jitterbug contests, been thrown
in the back of a paddy wagon, been struck by a car.

It's been battered by the first man I married.
And raped by a stranger
left me hooded, tied up, in a closet.
It's crawled in blackness to the face of a mine,
and changed the diaper of my best friend
after multiple sclerosis ravaged her.

This body's hands, whose fingers are tending east
and west, knuckles bumping out,
have fed the birds, and written books.
They play the lowliest instrument, the kazoo,
which takes only tune and breath and amplifies
the human voice! in rowdy exaltation.

About the author

Suzanne Rhodenbaugh is the author of poetry books *Lick of Sense* and *The Whole Shebang,* four chapbooks, and the essay collection *The Deepest South I've Gotten.* Her poems, essays, articles and reviews have been widely published in periodicals, including *The American Scholar, The Hudson Review, Michigan Quarterly Review, Poetry East, Salmagundi* and *The Washington Post;* and in anthologies by Columbia University Press, Black Sparrow Press and others.

She earned degrees from University of South Florida, University of Michigan and Vermont College. She's worked as an administrator and consultant in poverty and labor health programs, a book reviewer and writing teacher, a community organizer, and a full-time stepmother.

Her literary papers are in the Suzanne Wadley Jaworski Rhodenbaugh Papers, 1961-present, Special Collections, University of South Florida Library in Tampa.

With her husband Tom and their grandson David she lives in St. Louis.

www.ingramcontent.com/pod-product-compliance
Lightning Source LLC
Chambersburg PA
CBHW030650190726
48286CB00008B/2755